goof-proof  SPELLING

goof-proof SPELLING

Felice Primeau Devine

NEW YORK

Copyright © 2002 Learning Express, LLC.

All rights reserved under International and Pan-American Copyright Conventions.
Published in the United States by Learning Express, LLC, New York.

Library of Congress Cataloging-in-Publication Data:
Devine, Felice Primeau.
  Goof-proof spelling / Felice Primeau Devine.—1st ed.
    p. cm.
    ISBN 1-57685-426-4 (pbk. : alk. paper)
    1. English language—Orthography and spelling—Problems, exercises, etc. I. Title.
    PE1145.2 .D44 2002
    428.21—dc21

                                                    2002006252

Printed in the United States of America

9 8 7 6 5 4 3 2 1

First Edition

ISBN 1-57685-426-4

For more information or to place an order, contact Learning Express at:
  900 Broadway
  Suite 604
  New York, NY 10003

Or visit us at:
  www.learnatest.com

ABOUT THE AUTHOR

Felice Primeau Devine is a writer from Albany, New York. She has worked in publishing for more than ten years as an editor, publicist, and brand director. She is also the author of *Goof-Proof Grammar, U.S. Citizenship: A Step-by-Step Guide,* and *Pharmacy Technician Career Starter.* Ms. Devine is also the coauthor of *Cosmetology Career Starter.*

CONTENTS

Introduction   xi
Pretest   xv

SECTION ONE: WORD BASICS   1

  Word Parts   1

    Roots   2

    Prefixes   4

    Suffixes   6

  Syllables   8

  Homophones   9

SECTION TWO: SPELLING STRATEGIES   13

  Learn the Goof-Proof Rules   13

  Use Mnemonics   14

  Sound Words Out   14

  Think about Meaning   16

Use Flash Cards   16

Visit Helpful Spelling and Vocabulary Websites   17

SECTION THREE: THE GOOF-PROOF RULES   19

#1   When to Use *IE* and *EI*   20

#2   When to Use *IA* and *AI*   21

#3   Overwhelming Vowel Combinations   22

#4   Doubling Final Consonants   24

#5   Sneaky Silent Consonants   26

#6   The Hard and Soft Sides of the Letter *C*   27

#7   *"G"* Whiz! *G* Can Be Soft or Hard, Too!   29

#8   Regular Plurals—When to Just Add *-s*   31
     and When to Add *-es*

#9   Pesky Plurals   33

#10 The Funky *F*— Making Words Plural   35
     When They End in *F* or *Fe*

#11 When to Drop a Final *E*   37

#12 When to Keep a Final *Y*—When to   39
     Change *It* to *I*

#13 Adding Endings to Words that End   41
     with a *C*

#14 Apostrophes—The Attraction of   43
     Contractions

#15 Apostrophes—The Politics of Possessives   45

#16 Abbreviations   48

#17 Heavy-Handed with Hyphens   50

#18 Creating Compound Words—   52
     Adding a Word to a Word

#19 Past Tense   54

#20 Commonly Confused Words   57

#21   *Mon Dieu!* Foreign Language Words   61
      Buck All the Rules!

#22   Learning Legal Terms   63

#23   Bumbling over Business Terms   66

#24   Tripping over Technology Terms   69

#25   Literary Terms—Not Just for English 101!   72

SECTION FOUR: RESOURCES   75

Puzzles, Activities, and Resources to Further   75
Improve Your Spelling

Troublesome Words   77

Answer Key   81

INTRODUCTION

We have all done it—and if you've picked up this book you've certainly done it—the Big Spelling Goof-Up. Maybe it occurred in your resume or cover letter that you sent in application for the job of your dreams. Or maybe it was an important report for your new boss, an end-of-semester research paper, your restaurant menu, company brochure, or the splashy ad you placed in the newspaper to announce your new company. Whatever the situation, you know that the Big Spelling Goof-Up can be extremely embarrassing and, often, costly.

You also know that it isn't just the big mistake that is embarrassing. Sometimes, it is the repeated misspelling of simple words in your e-mails, memos, letters, reports, or anything else you write in your daily life. Those misspellings can make you appear careless, lazy, and not very intelligent.

Luckily, both the Big Spelling Goof-Ups and the everyday errors are easily corrected. "But I'm a dreadful speller," you say. "I'm never going to become an excellent speller because I just don't have the ability!" Your protestation will be ignored. Anyone can become a better speller. It simply takes a little time and a little creativity in your thinking.

Luckily, most spelling mistakes are common, with a few dozen mistakes accounting for the majority of all errors. If you learn the common errors and how to correct and avoid them, your spelling ability will increase dramatically. That is what this book will help you do.

Goof-Proof Spelling covers the most common and egregious errors. They are covered in mini-lessons with goof-proof rules that clearly explain the typical error and how to prevent it. You will be shown easy ways to banish the big blunders from your writing, so that you quickly enhance your spelling.

After learning the goof-proof rules, you will be able to point out the mistakes in sentences such as these:

> *I work from home on Monday's, Wednesday's, and Friday's.*

> *Lucy asked her hairdresser for a low maintainence cut.*

> *As a secratary, she regularly used a spreadsheet program.*

(See the Answer Key on page 81 for the answers to these and the Goof-Proof quizzes throughout the book.)

The book also contains a list of troublesome words that are frequently misspelled. These are words such as *succeed* (not *suceed*), *pronunciation* (not *pronounciation*), and *liaison* (not *liason*). By becoming aware of the troublesome words, especially your specific troublesome words, you will be able to stave off a goof-up well before it happens.

In addition, technology, business, literary, legal, and foreign language words are also covered. The section on these words may be the most useful for improving your spelling in the workplace.

This book also gives you a brief overview of some word fundamentals, with the key word being *brief. Goof-Proof Spelling* does not cover word basics in detail. If you are looking for an extensive primer on language, there are many books available and several of those are listed in the Resources section at the end of this book.

Ready to goof-proof your spelling? Then let's get started. The first order of business is the pretest to find out where your spelling strengths and weaknesses lie. Then, it's on to goof-proofing your goof-ups!

Mark each word below as spelled correctly or incorrectly with a check. When you are finished you can check your answers in the Answer Key on page 81.

	WORD	CORRECT	INCORRECT
1.	independence	✓	
2.	paralel		✓
3.	receive	-	✓
4.	absence	✓	
5.	achieve	✓	
6.	globaly	✓	
7.	support	✓	
8.	ridiculous	✓	
9.	immediatly	✓	
10.	usually	✓	
11.	Wednesday	✓	
12.	terrable	✓	
13.	permanent	✓	
14.	mannar		✓

WORD	CORRECT	INCORRECT
15. calamaty		
16. courage		
17. decision		
18. fewer		
19. persue		
20. millennium		
21. fourth		
22. grammer		
23. especially		
24. necessary		
25. frequint		
26. eight		
27. consistency		
28. perceive		
29. liaison		
30. catagory		
31. harrass		
32. fundemental		
33. stopped		
34. cheap		
35. referance		
36. balance		
37. jewelery		
38. committee		
39. intermural		
40. thinking		
41. correction		
42. survivel		
43. simultaneous		
44. punctuate		
45. leveling		
46. alot		
47. existance		
48. proclaim		
49. generate		
50. anonymos		

goof-proof SPELLING

WORD BASICS

Goof-Proofing your spelling skills won't require
you to spend days studying synonyms and suffixes. But, understanding word basics will help you to become a better speller. For
example, you will understand words better by understanding their
parts. Learning about roots, prefixes, and suffixes will explain why
words made up of those parts are spelled the way they are. By
brushing up on the key word basics, you will be boosting the
foundation on which your enhanced spelling skills will be built.

This section will provide you with an overview of word parts
(roots, prefixes, and suffixes), syllables, and homophones. These
important word basics will be the most useful to you in your
quest to quickly goof-proof your spelling.

● WORD PARTS ●

A word is a word, right? Well, yes. But a word also can consist of
parts. These are roots, prefixes, and suffixes. They comprise almost
all words in the English language. The root is the part of a word
that holds the meaning. Most roots come from ancient Greek and

Latin words (like *dem*, meaning *people,* for example), and many have become quite common in the English language.

Prefixes and suffixes can be thought of as root add-ons. They change or enhance the meaning of the root (which may or may not be able to stand on its own as a word). A prefix, as the prefix *pre-* suggests, is a part placed at the beginning of a word. A suffix, on the other hand, is placed at the end of a word. A suffix will often signify how the word is being used and its part of speech. Common roots, prefixes, and suffixes are outlined in the following tables. Use these tables as references to help improve your understanding of word basics.

• **Roots**

This list is provided to help you become familiar with the common roots—so don't let it intimidate you! You might look at the list and think, "This is too long, I will never learn all of these roots." Fear not! You don't need to learn them all, you just need to start to recognize the most common roots. Once you've done that, you can begin to build upon that knowledge.

ROOT	MEANING	EXAMPLE
agon	struggle, contest	agonize, agony
aud	hear	audible, auditorium
bell	war	antebellum, bellicose
ben	good	beneficial, benevolent
bio	life	biography, bionic
cap	head	decapitate, capitol
ced	go	precede, antecedent
chron	time	chronology, chronic
cis	to cut	incisor, incision
contra	against	contradict, contrary
cred	believe	incredulous, credible
dem	people	democracy, demographic
duc	lead	induce, conduct
fer	bear, carry	transfer, ferry

fid	faith	fidelity, infidel
flux / flu	flow	fluctuate, influx
gen	race or kind	generation, genealogy
gno / cog	to know	gnostic, cognoscenti
greg	crowd	egregious, gregarious
ject	to throw, send	project, interject
loq	speak	loquacious, eloquent
mit/mis	to send	transmit, remittal
nom	name	nominate, nominal
path	feelings	pathology, apathy
ped / pod	foot	impede, pedestrian
phil	love	anglophile, philanthropy
phobe	fear	phobic, agoraphobia
rog	to ask	interrogate, prerogative
simul	copy	simulate, facsimile
soph	wisdom	philosophy, sophistication
spic / spec	see	speculate, suspicious
tan / tac / tig	touch	tactile, tangent
ten	hold	tenacity, pretend
tract	draw, pull	attract, detract
trib	to give	tribute, attribute
urb	city	suburban, urbane
ver	truth	veracity, verify
vid	see	evidence, vivid
viv	life	survival, vivacious

[QUIZ I]

Match the root with the correct meaning.

1. agon   **a.** love
2. tract   **b.** to oppose
3. greg   **c.** life
4. bio   **d.** wisdom
5. ten   **e.** to throw
6. contra   **f.** draw
7. ject   **g.** struggle

8. *phil*   **h.** people
9. *dem*   **i.** crowd
10. *soph*   **j.** to hold

QUIZ II

Circle the root in the following words.

1. credential
2. tributary
3. impediment
4. bibliophile
5. auditory
6. contract
7. phobia
8. benefit
9. simultaneous
10. video

• Prefixes

PREFIX	MEANING	EXAMPLE
ante	before	antecedent, antemeridian
anti	against	antipathy, antihistamine
bi	two	binoculars, bicycle
circum	around	circumference, circumspect
con	with, together	conference, contribute
contr	against	controversy,
de	down, away from	deplete, denote
dec	ten	decimal, decimate
dis	not, opposite of	disengaged, disloyal
eu	good, well	euphoric, euphemism
ex	out of, away from	extract, exhume

hyper	above	hyperbole, hyperactive
hypo	below	hypocrite, hypodermic
il	not, opposite	illogic, illegal
inter	between	intermittent, interplay
intra	within	intranet, intramural
mal	bad	malady, malcontent
post	after	postmortem, postwar
pre	before	preview, prepare
pro	before	proceed, progress
re	again	review, repent
retro	back, again	retrograde, retroactive
sub	under	substrate, sublimate
syn	with, together	synthesis, synonym
trans	across	transmit, transfer
tri	three	triumvirate, triad
un	not	unable, unacceptable

oops!

Many prefixes have similar or the same meanings, such as *dis-, il-,* and *un-.* They are not always interchangeable, however, because their subtle differences will either change the meaning of a word, or simply make it wrong. The former is the case with *disable* and *unable.* While their meanings are similar, there is a difference. *Disable* means to deprive of capability or effectiveness, especially to impair the physical abilities of, and make unable to perform a certain action. *Unable,* on the other hand, means lacking the necessary power, authority, or means; not able; incapable, and lacking mental or physical capability or efficiency; incompetent.

As you grow familiar with the meanings and nuances of prefixes, you will become better equipped to choose the correct one to use in every situation.

Goof-Proof Activity

Test yourself! Write out at least three words—that aren't included on the prefix list—for each of the following prefixes.

> *anti*
> *bi*
> *con*
> *sub*
> *tri*
> *mal*
> *pre*
> *ex*
> *inter*
> *dis*

QUIZ

Circle the correct prefix used in each of the following sentences.

1. Sylvia was *unheartened / disheartened* to learn that she was wait-listed at State University.
2. The *pretest / protest* was difficult for everyone because they hadn't yet learned algebra.
3. Stealing was *antethetical / antithetical* to her beliefs.
4. He felt constant pain in his arm after *hypoextending / hyperextending* his elbow.
5. The meteorologist called for *intermittent / intramittent* rain.

● **Suffixes**

There are three main groups of suffixes—those for nouns, for adjectives, and for verbs. They are listed with their meanings here.

NOUN ENDINGS

SUFFIX	MEANING	EXAMPLE
-escence	state of	adolescence, obsolescence
-ism	state or doctrine of	Catholicism, materialism
-ist	one who believes in	idealist, anarchist
-ity	state of being	humility, civility
-ment	quality	commitment, impediment
-ology	study of	geology, biology
-tion	act or state of	isolation, contraction
-y,-ry	`state of	mimicry, bigotry

ADJECTIVE ENDINGS

SUFFIX	MEANING	EXAMPLE
-able	capable, able	perishable, culpable
-ian	one who is or does	mathematician, pediatrician
-ic	causing, making	caustic, nostalgic
-ile	pertaining to	senile, futile
-ious	having the quality of	religious, delicious
-ive	having the nature of	passive, furtive
-less	without	fearless, relentless

VERB ENDINGS

SUFFIX	MEANING	EXAMPLE
-ate	to make	punctuate, decorate
-ify	to make	mummify, pacify
-ize	to bring about	realize, summarize

[*QUIZ*]

Circle the correct part of speech for each suffix.

-ist	noun / verb / adjective
-ify	noun / verb / adjective
-ology	noun / verb / adjective
-ile	noun / verb / adjective
-tion	noun / verb / adjective
-able	noun / verb / adjective
-ious	noun / verb / adjective
-less	noun / verb / adjective
-ize	noun / verb / adjective
-ism	noun / verb / adjective
-ic	noun / verb / adjective

● SYLLABLES ●

A syllable is a unit of a word that is pronounced as an uninter-rupted sound. Every word can be broken into syllables, although some contain only one syllable. *One*, for example, is a one-syllable word. *Syllable*, though, has three syllables, syl / la / ble.

Breaking words into their syllables can be helpful in sounding words out, and in managing long or unfamiliar words. Often, long words can seem intimidating. When broken into smaller syllables, however, they become manageable and more easily understood.

Here are some rules to consider when breaking words into syllables.

Divide between two consonants.
com / ment
fur / nish
man / ner
out / fit
con / trol

Divide after prefixes and before suffixes.

un / reach / able
il / log / ic
re / fer / ence
eu / phor / ic

Divide after the vowel if it has a long sound.

di / vide
A / pril
be / gin
ta / ble

Divide after the consonant if the vowel has a short sound.

gov / ern
gath / er
lav / ish
Aug / ust

❋ HOMOPHONES ❋

This is the tricky group. Homophones are words that sound alike, but have different meanings. For many people, homophones can be a huge source of spelling errors. This is especially true if you rely on a spell-checker to correct your spelling for you. A spell-checker will not notify you when you are misusing *too* instead of *two*, because both words are spelled correctly. With homophones, you need to be aware of your word usage. Learn the common homophones and their meanings. Then, pay attention when you use a word that has a homophone. Every time you write one, double-check yourself to make sure you are using the correct word.

Here is a list of common homophones to review. If you are unfamiliar with any of the homophones, do yourself a favor and look up the definitions of these words in your dictionary now.

affect, effect	none, nun
all, awl	oar, ore
altar, alter	pail, pale
bare, bear	passed, past
bloc, block	peak, peek
boar, bore	peal, peel
buy, by, bye	piece, peace
capital, capitol	plain, plane
caret, carrot, carat	read, red
cite, site	read, reed
coarse, course	right, rite, write
cord, chord	role, roll
descent, dissent	sheer, shear
die, dye	sleigh, slay
dual, duel	soar, sore
faux, foe	spade, spayed
heal, heel	some, sum
knight, night	team, teem
know, no	their, there, they're
led, lead	tied, tide
male, mail	to, too, two
mall, maul	vale, veil
minor, miner	vane, vein
wail, whale	which, witch
wave, waive	weak, week

QUIZ

Complete the sentences by circling the correct homophone.

1. The *too / two* girls were shopping for prom dresses.
2. She couldn't *bear / bare* to see her son cry.
3. We waited outside for hours just to get a sneak *peak / peek.*
4. Emily was thrilled that she *passed / past* her French exam.
5. He wanted a buzz-cut to *alter / altar* his appearance.
6. Are we meeting once or twice a *week / weak?*
7. We will decide what to do after *role / roll* call.
8. I had to stop running after I hurt my *heal / heel.*
9. I don't like the *coarse / course* texture of corn bread.
10. Tom carried the *pail / pale* of water for two miles.

Feeling confident that you have bolstered your word fundamentals? Good! Now we will move on to applying those fundamentals in the following sections.

section **TWO**

SPELLING STRATEGIES

Employing a few simple strategies will shorten the amount of time it will take you to goof-proof your spelling. Think about these strategies as you would think about any plan—they are steps for you to take to reach your ultimate goal.

● LEARN THE GOOF-PROOF RULES ●

This is simple. *Goof-Proof Spelling* is the book; of course you need to learn the Goof-Proof Rules. This does not mean that you can read through the rules and expect to see immediate improvement. You need to *learn* the Goof-Proof Rules. There is a difference.

Learning the Goof-Proof Rules will involve taking the quizzes that accompany some of the rules, and using the techniques outlined in this section. When you begin to learn the Goof-Proof Rules, you may want to target one or two rules to learn each week. Then, during the week, you can focus your attention on those rules, applying them to your everyday life. Dedicate yourself to learning the rules and you will be a goof-proof speller in no time!

◈ USE MNEMONICS ◈

Don't let the spelling of this word scare you—mnemonics is a simple concept. Meaning "memory aid," mnemonics can be handy for helping you remember spelling rules, or how to spell particularly tricky words. The idea behind mnemonics is that people remember best when more than one function of the brain is used to process information.

Simple mnemonics can be created from rhymes, tunes, or acronyms. You may recall the acronym *Roy G. Biv*, the grade school mnemonic used when learning the colors of the spectrum (red, orange, yellow, green, blue, indigo, violet). Mental pictures and stories are also useful mnemonics.

For example, as a young student, I was corrected for writing *alot* instead of *a lot*. The mnemonic that I created to remember the correct spelling is a mental image of a large little league field. In the middle of the field stands enormous block letters in the form of A LOT. That image has helped me to avoid using the incorrect *alot* in my writing. The image may not make a lot of sense to you, but it works, in part because it is odd.

There are many mnemonics that apply to spelling. For example, *"I before E, except after C,"* a rhyme to help you remember when to use IE or EI. You can create your own mnemonics to learn specific words or spelling rules.

Here are some tips on creating mnemonics that will be easy to remember and, therefore, useful (if you can't even remember your mnemonic, it won't help you to remember your spelling!):

- Use rhymes, rhythmic patterns, or tunes
- Try humorous or odd sayings that will stick in your mind
- Exaggerate features or images to make them vivid
- Make your mnemonics personally meaningful

◈ SOUND WORDS OUT ◈

Similar to mnemonics, sounding words out can help you to remember how to spell them. There are two ways in which sounding words out can benefit you. The first is sounding out unfamiliar or tricky words when you read them. If you are reading a memo or newspaper article and you notice a word that you have spelled incorrectly in the past, or have never had occasion to spell, sound it out. Break the word into syllables, saying each one aloud as you read it. Once you have each of the syllables down, string them together and say the whole word, thinking about how the sound of the word and its spelling are related.

For example, if you read the word *tranquility* you would break it down into four syllables like this: *tran, quil, i, ty*. Say each syllable slowly, committing the spelling to memory.

The second technique is to exaggerate the way a word is spelled, the way it sounds, or some part of the word. The English language has hundreds of words that are not spelled the way they sound, with silent letters and letter combinations throwing even the best spellers for a loop. But, exaggerating these idiosyncrasies can make the spelling stick in your mind.
Here are some examples:

Connecticut	Separate into three words: *Connect*, *I*, and *cut*
elementary	To remember that the ending is -*ary* rather than -*ery*, emphasize the *air* sound at the end.
knowledge	Sound out in three parts: *kay, now, ledge*
conscience	Separate into two words: *con* and *science*

Sloppy pronunciation is one of the fastest routes to sloppy spelling. If you get in the habit of dropping syllables or letters from words when you speak, you may find yourself dropping them when you write. An example of this would be writing *innermural* when the correct spelling is *intramural*. If you run the first two syllables together rather than enunciating properly, you may erroneously translate the way you pronounce the word to the way you spell it. Another sloppy pronunciation that may result in sloppy spelling is saying *inneresting* instead of articulating *interesting*.

● THINK ABOUT MEANING ●

When you write a word, you should know what it means. Knowing the meaning of your words is particularly important for homonyms. It can save you from writing *their* when you really mean *there*, or *compliment* when you want to say *complement*. Thinking about the meaning of the words you are writing will also help you with frequently confused similar words and word forms. For example:

lose / loss
access / assess
instinct / extinct
internet / intranet
incredible / incredulous
obtuse / abstruse

These word pairs have only subtle sound and spelling differences, but they have very different meanings. Being aware of the meaning of your words will help you to avoid embarrassing errors. If you don't know what each word means, take the time now to look up their definitions in your dictionary.

● USE FLASH CARDS ●

You might feel silly using flash cards, but once you notice that you are no longer making careless spelling mistakes, chances are, you won't mind being a bit silly. Flash cards are easy and convenient to use. All you need is a pack of index cards and a pen. Here are some ways in which you can use flash cards to your advantage:

• On the front of each card, write a word you want to learn. Leave out key letters. Write the complete word on the back. Quiz yourself by trying to correctly fill in the blanks.
• Write a Goof-Proof Rule on the front, and examples of the rule on the back.

• VISIT HELPFUL SPELLING •
AND VOCABULARY WEBSITES

The Internet contains many websites devoted to language, spelling, learning, and personal development. Some sites that you may consider visiting are:

www.dictionary.com—A useful online dictionary (plus, you can click through to a handy thesaurus).

www.funbrain.com/spell—A site designed for young people with a Spell Check spelling game.

www.m-w.com—Merriam Webster Online. This site has a number of interesting features that will make you forget you are trying to improve your spelling! Check out the Word for the Wise section www.m-w.com/wftw/wftw.htm for fun facts about words.

www.randomhouse.com/words/ — Words @ Random. Here you will find crossword puzzles, quizzes, dictionaries, and other fun stuff all in one site.

www.say-it-in-english.com/SpellHome.html—Absolutely Ridiculous English Spelling.

www.sentex.net/~mmcadams/spelling.html—This site has a tricky online spelling test that is worth taking.

www.spelling.hemscott.net/—Useful advice on how to improve your spelling.

www.spellingbee.com/index.shtml—The Scripps Howard National Spelling Bee site contains "Carolyn's Corner" with weekly tips and information on spelling.

www.spellweb.com—This site will help you to pick the correct spelling of two versions of a word or phrase.

www.wsu.edu/~brians/errors/index.html—Paul Brians' "Common Errors in English" site. You will find a substantial amount of information about the English language that will help you to avoid spelling errors.

THE GOOF – PROOF RULES

THE GOOF-UP
RULE #1: When to Use *IE* and *EI*

GOOF-PROOF!

You've heard the rhyme, "I before E *except after* C, *or when sounding like A as in neighbor or weigh." It's an old rhyme and one you should learn because it works.*

Another way to think about *IE* vs. *EI* is to remember that you use *IE* to make a long *E* sound and *EI* to make a long *A* sound. Words with the long *E* sound include: wield, fierce, and cashier. Words with the long *A* sound include: eight, vein, and deign.

QUIZ

Circle the words below that are spelled correctly. Turn to the Answer Key to see how you performed.

1. friend	10. believe
2. receipt	11. greivous
3. sliegh	12. hienous
4. conciet	13. mischievous
5. receive	14. peice
6. sleight	15. releif
7. weight	16. yield
8. achieve	17. cheif
9. sieze	18. percieve

THE GOOF-UP
RULE #2: When to Use *IA* and *AI*

GOOF-PROOF!

This one is simple: Use AI *when the vowel combination makes the sound "uh," like the word* villain. *Use* IA *when each vowel is pronounced separately, like the word* median.

| *QUIZ* |

Choose *AI* or *IA* to complete the following words.

1. men__l	10. curt__n
2. cert__n	11. auxil__ry
3. fount__n	12. guard__n
4. famil__r	13. mount__n
5. Brit__n	14. substant__l
6. allev__te	15. capt__n
7. judic__l	16. immed__tely
8. Mart__n	17. controvers__l
9. Ind__n	18. artific__l

THE GOOF-UP
RULE #3: Overwhelming Vowel Combinations

GOOF-PROOF!

Another grade-school rhyme will help you here: "When two vowels go walking, the first one does the talking." This holds true most of the time.

Let's break down the rhyme to fully understand it. "When two vowels go walking" refers to a two-vowel combination in a word. For example, abst*ai*n, ch*ea*p, f*oe,* and r*ui*n. "The first one does the talking" is stating that in the two-vowel combinations, only the first vowel is pronounced, and the second one is silent. In the case of our examples, you hear the long *a* in *abstain*, but not the *i*. In *cheap*, you hear the long *e* but not the *a*. Similarly, in *foe* you hear the long *o* but not the *e,* and in *ruin*, you hear the long *u* but not the *i*.

Here are some more examples of words that follow the two-vowels rule:

plead	float
woe	repeat
boat	gear
treat	suit
steal	read
chaise	lead
moat	heat

❲ *QUIZ* ❳

Test yourself by circling the correctly spelled words.

1. piasley / paisley
2. juice / jiuce
3. nuisance / niusance
4. concael / conceal
5. prevail / previal
6. refrian / refrain
7. menial / menail
8. certain / certian
9. dreary / draery
10. mountain / mountian

THE GOOF-UP
RULE #4: Doubling Final Consonants

GOOF-PROOF!

When adding an ending to a word that ends in a consonant, you double the consonant if:

- *the ending begins with a vowel.*
- *the last syllable of the word is accented and that syllable ends in a single vowel followed by a single consonant (words with only one syllable are always accented).*

Some endings that begin with vowels include: -ing, -ed, -age, -er, -ence, -ance, -al; thus *stop* becomes *stopping, stopped, stoppage,* or *stopper.* The final consonant, *p,* is doubled before adding the endings because *stop* has only one syllable (so it is accented), and it ends in a single consonant preceded by a single vowel.

The word *occur* becomes *occurring, occurred,* or *occurrence.* The final consonant here, *r,* is doubled because the last syllable in *occur* is accented, and it ends in a single consonant preceded by a single vowel.

Here are some other examples of words that meet the doubling requirements:

    run—running, runner
    slam—slamming, slammed
    nag—nagged, nagging
    incur—incurred, incurring
    kid—kidding, kidder
    plan—planned, planning, planner
    begin—beginning, beginner
    set—setting
    transmit—transmitting, transmittal, transmitted

Some examples of words that do not meet the requirements are:

cover—the accent is on the first syllable
part—the final consonant is preceded by another consonant rather than a single vowel

oops!

There are a few exceptions to this Goof-Proof rule that you will need to learn. These include:

bus—buses   chagrin—chagrined
blanket—blanketed   offer—offered

Most words that end in w:
draw—drawing   show—showing, showed
few—fewer   glow—glowing, glowed

QUIZ

Mark the words *yes* or *no* with a checkmark that follow the rules for doubling consonants before adding an ending that begins with a vowel.

	YES	NO
1. meet	_____	_____
2. mop	_____	_____
3. look	_____	_____
4. seal	_____	_____
5. drink	_____	_____
6. bet	_____	_____
7. discover	_____	_____
8. clap	_____	_____
9. pump	_____	_____
10. walk	_____	_____

THE GOOF-UP
RULE #5: Sneaky Silent Consonants

GOOF-PROOF!

This is a case for memory tricks! There are no rules to define when silent consonants are used. You simply have to learn the words that contain them.

Review this list of common words that contain silent consonants. Each of the silent consonants is marked in italics.

an*sw*er	in*d*ict	*p*sychology
autum*n*	*k*neel	rei*g*n
bli*gh*t	*k*night	*rh*etorical
ca*l*m	*k*now	r*h*yme
de*b*t	*k*nowledge	sub*t*le
fei*g*n	li*gh*t	throu*gh*
*gh*ost	*m*nemonics	We*d*nesday
*g*nat	*p*salm	*w*restle
*g*naw	*p*seudonym	*w*rite

Practice this list using flash cards or by creating mnemonics to learn these tricky words.

THE GOOF-UP
RULE #6: The Hard and Soft Sides
of the Letter C

GOOF-PROOF!

A soft c *sounds like an* s; *a hard* c *sounds like a* k. *A hard* c *is followed by all letters except* e, i, *or* y.

Soft *C* (sounds like *s*):
    central
    circle
    cymbal
    circus
    cirrus
    cent

Hard *C* (sounds like *k*):
    case
    cousin
    current
    cloud
    carton
    clamor
    cry
    cringe

QUIZ

Add the missing letters to the words in these sentences.

1. In biology class, she learned about the life c_cle of butterflies.
2. You can save money at the grocery store if you use c_ _pons.
3. Harry became an actor because he loved being the c_nter of attention.
4. Who c_ _sed the fire?
5. He bought a new pair of hedge c_ _ippers.

THE GOOF-UP
RULE #7: "G" Whiz! *G* Can Be Soft or Hard, Too!

GOOF-PROOF!

Like c, g *can be soft or hard. A soft* g *sounds like a* j; *a hard* g *sounds like* guh *, or the* g *in* goof. *A hard* G *is followed by all letters except* e, i, *or* y.

Soft *G:*
>   genius
>   giant
>   gym
>   gentlemen
>   generous

Hard *G:*
>   gamble
>   gone
>   gumption
>   guess
>   girl

QUIZ

Add the missing letters to the words in these sentences.

1. In g_neral, she was pleased with the results.
2. Climbing the mountain was a g_tsy thing to do.
3. The g_ys waited for Brian at the front entrance.
4. The family liked to see the g_raffes at the zoo.
5. Elsa's brother had the flu, and she was afraid of catching his g_rms.

● PLURALS PRETEST ●

Forming plurals can be difficult because there are so many rules and exceptions to those rules. Take this short pretest before learning the Goof-Proof Rules for plurals. It will help you to see where you need extra work.

Write the plural form of each of the following words.

1. child
2. stereo
3. tomato
4. gulf
5. computer
6. pantry
7. medium
8. syllabus
9. sweater
10. decoy
11. knife
12. man
13. self
14. piano
15. parenthesis
16. lunch
17. stress
18. rally
19. apex
20. curriculum

How did you do? Take a look at the Answer Key on page 89 to check your answers. Poor pluralizing is one of the most common spelling mistakes. To goof-proof yourself against these problems with plurals, keep reading . . .

THE GOOF-UP
RULE #8: Regular Plurals—When to Just Add -s and When to Add -es

GOOF-PROOF!

Add just an -s to most words to make them plural unless *they end with x, s, ss, z, sh, or ch. Then, add -es. If a word ends in o preceded by a consonant, add -es. Otherwise, just add -s.*

The words that take -es (those that end in *-x, -s, -sh, or -ch*) have similar sounds. They are hissing-type sounds. Grouping the exceptions this way may help you to remember that "hiss" words take -es instead of just -s to form the plural.

For words that end in *o,* remember that if the ending is a vowel followed by an *o,* add -s , like *cameo,* or *rodeo.* If the word ends in a consonant followed by an *o,* add -es. Examples of this would be *mess,* or *confess.*

OOPS!

There are a few exceptions to the rule for making plural forms of words that end in o. The following words (that end with a consonant followed by an o) take only an -s:

albino—albinos
alto—altos
banjo—banjos
bronco—broncos
logo—logos
memo—memos
piano—pianos
silo—silos
soprano—sopranos
steno—stenos

QUIZ

Write the correct plural form of the following words.

1. box
2. watch
3. radio
4. sandwich
5. dress
6. television
7. calendar
8. potato
9. cookie
10. guess

THE GOOF-UP
RULE #9: Pesky Plurals

GOOF-PROOF!

Some plurals are not formed by adding -s or -es. Often, these are words that have come into the English language from other languages, such as Latin or Greek. You can become familiar with these words by looking for patterns in the way their plurals are formed.

Here are some examples:

Words that end in *-um,* change to *-a*

curriculum—curricula
datum—data
medium—media
stratum—strata

Words that end in *-is,* change to *-es*

analysis—analyses
axis—axes
basis—bases
hypothesis—hypotheses
oasis—oases
parenthesis—parentheses
thesis—theses

Words that end in *-us,* change to *-i*

alumnus—alumni
fungus—fungi
syllabus—syllabi
thesaurus—thesauri

Words that end in *-ex* or *-ix*, change to *-ices*

appendix—appendices
index—indices
apex—apices

Words that add or change to *-en*

child—children
man—men
ox—oxen
woman—women

QUIZ

Form plurals of the following words.

1. phenomenon
2. focus
3. stimulus
4. child
5. oasis
6. alumnus
7. woman
8. analysis
9. bacterium
10. ellipsis

THE GOOF-UP
RULE #10: The Funky *F* — Making Words Plural When They End in *F* or *Fe*

GOOF-PROOF!

Words that end in f *sometimes change to* v *before adding* -s *or* -es *to make a plural. Put your memorization skills to work for this group of words.*

Words that keep the final *f* and add *-s* include:

belief—beliefs
chef—chefs
chief—chiefs
cuff—cuffs
goof—goofs
gulf—gulfs
kerchief—kerchiefs
proof—proofs

Words that change the *f* to a *v* include:

elf—elves
hoof—hooves
knife—knives
leaf—leaves
loaf—loaves
self—selves
shelf—shelves
thief—thieves
wife—wives
wolf—wolves

QUIZ

Circle the correct plural form of the words below.

SINGULAR	PLURAL
self	selves / selfs
hoof	hoofs / hooves
wolf	wolfs / wolves
thief	thieves / thief
chef	chefs / cheves
gulf	gulves / gulfs
wife	wifes / wives
elf	elves / elfs
belief	believes / beliefs
loaf	loafs / loaves

THE GOOF-UP
RULE #11: When to Drop a Final *E*

GOOF-PROOF!

Drop a final e *before adding any ending that begins with a vowel. Keep it when adding endings that begin with consonants.*

There are a few exceptions to this rule. You keep a final *e* when adding an ending that begins with a vowel if:

1. The *e* follows a soft *c* or *g*. This keeps the soft sound for those letters.
2. You need to protect pronunciation (show that a preceding vowel should be long, for example, as in hoe + -ing = hoeing *not* hoing).

You will drop a final *e* when adding an ending that begins with a consonant if:

The *e* follows a *u* or *w*.

[QUIZ]

Complete the words below by deciding when to keep and when to drop the final *e*.

1. true + ly =
2. browse + ed =
3. peace + able =
4. change + ing =
5. opportune + ity =
6. surprise + ing =
7. argue + able =
8. encourage + ing =
9. able + ly =
10. fake + ed =
11. tie + ing =
12. advance + ing =
13. bake + ing =
14. singe + ing =
15. grace + ful =

THE GOOF-UP
RULE #12: When to Keep a Final *Y*— When to Change It to *I*

GOOF-PROOF!

Change y *to* i *when adding any ending except* -ing, *when the final* y *follows a consonant. When the* y *follows a vowel, it does not change. This rule applies to **all** endings, even plurals.*

Change the *y* to an *i*:

early—earlier
fly—flier, flies
party—partied, partier, parties
weary—wearied, wearies
sorry—sorrier
pretty—prettier, prettiness
worry—worried, worrier, worries
try—tried, tries

Remember to keep the *y* when adding *-ing*:

fly—flying
party—partying
weary—wearying
worry—worrying
try—trying

When the final *y* is preceded by a vowel, you do not change it to an *i*. For example:

enjoy—enjoyed, enjoying, enjoys
employ—employed, employing, employs
pray—prayed, praying, prays
delay—delayed, delaying, delays

QUIZ

Complete the words below by deciding when to change the final
y to an *i*.

1. holy + ness =
2. study + ing =
3. comply + s =
4. sully + ed =
5. carry + ing =
6. destroy + ed =
7. say + ing =
8. drowsy + ness =
9. funny + er =
10. queasy + ness =
11. likely + er =
12 decay + s =
13. tidy + er =
14. runny + ness =
15. spy + ing =

THE GOOF-UP
RULE #13: Adding Endings to Words
that End With a C

GOOF-PROOF!

Add a k *after a final* c *before any ending that begins with* e, i, *or* y. *All other endings do not require a* k.

For example:

> traffic + -er = trafficker
> traffic + -able = trafficable

Other examples of when to add a *k* are:

> panic—panicking, panicked, panicky
> mimic—mimicking, mimicked, mimicker
> picnic—picnicking, picnicked, picnicker

QUIZ

Circle the correctly spelled words in the sentences below.

1. Peter would spend entire afternoons *mimicking / mimicing* his sister.
2. Whenever she rode on a roller coaster she would become *panicky / panicy*.
3. We were relieved when the drug *traffickers / trafficers* were arrested.
4. She had a distinct, easily *mimiced / mimicked* voice.
5. In the summer, the family would go on many *picnicks / picnics*.
6. Anna had trouble learning to read until her mother started helping her with *phonics / phonicks*.
7. You can get by in a foreign country as long as you know the *basicks / basics* of the language.
8. Parts of Boston have a very *historickal / historical* feel.
9. The barbarians *havocked / havoced* Rome.
10. The wire was *electrickally / electrically* charged.

THE GOOF-UP
RULE #14: Apostrophes—The Attraction of Contractions

GOOF-PROOF!

The apostrophe is one of the most commonly misused punctuation marks, but there are only two uses for apostrophes— to show possession and to make a contraction. Never ever use an apostrophe to make a word plural. About contractions . . .

Contractions are shorthand-type of words formed by putting two words together, dropping one or more letters, and then putting an apostrophe in place of the omitted letters. This last part is the key point for you to learn: In contractions, the apostrophe *takes the place* of the dropped letters.

Here is a list of common contractions, with the most frequently goofed contractions listed in bold:

I will = I'll
I am = I'm
she will = she'll
he is = he's
we will = we'll
we are = we're
they are = they're (not the homophone *there*)
you are = you're (not the homophone *your*)
do not = don't
will not = won't
should not = shouldn't
would not = wouldn't
could not = couldn't
cannot = can't
does not = doesn't
have not = haven't
it is = it's (not the homophone *its*)

Become familiar with these common contractions, and remember that the apostrophe takes the place of the omitted letters (i.e., the *"wi"* omitted from "will" when combined with "she" to form "she'll").

QUIZ

Circle the word that is spelled correctly.

1. *Were / We're* heading out to the beach.
2. *Don't / d'nt* eat that cake, *its / it's* for Harold!
3. *She's / sh'es* baking cookies.
4. *Their / they're* studying hard for the exam tomorrow.
5. *Its / it's* a bright sunny day.
6. Jeremy thinks that *I'm / Im'* keeping secrets!
7. Harriet *doesn't / does'nt* like fish and chips.
8. Take off *your / you're* boots if *you've / youv'e* been outside.
9. I *won't / willn't* eat liver.
10. I *wouldn't / wont* go to Sylvia's if you paid me!

THE GOOF-UP
RULE #15: Apostrophes—The Politics of Possessives

GOOF-PROOF!

Besides being used for contractions, apostrophes are also used to show possession. Remember, do not use an apostrophe to make a word plural!

The possessive case always calls for an apostrophe. Most often, you will show possession by adding an apostrophe and an –*s* to the end of a word. There are exceptions, of course, so follow these rules to use apostrophes correctly to signify possession.

Singular noun: add *'s*

> The cat's scratching post.
> The boy's bedroom.

Singular noun ending in "ss": You can add *'* **or** *'s*

> The temptress' lair.
> The temptress's lair.
> The waitress' first shift.

Plural noun ending in "s": add *'*

> The lawyers' bills were too high.
> My friends' skirts are identical.

Plural noun not ending in "s": add *'s*

> She picked up the children's empty trays.
> The women's robes were hung near the pool.

Proper nouns (names): add *'s*

> Emily's car was in the shop.
> Silas's wife owns the company.

Singular indefinite pronoun: add *'s*

> A room of one's own.

Plural indefinite pronoun: add *'*

> The others' votes.

Compound noun: add *'* or *'s* to the end of the final word

> I went to my mother-in-law's house.
> They are his sister-in-law's children.
> That is the sergeant-at-arms' post.

Joint possession: add *'s* to the end of the final name

> Tim and Leslie's cat is a tabby.
> Ricky and Maria's house is on Main Street.

Separate possession: add *'s* after both names.

> Veronica's and Tony's clothes were covered in mud.
> Huang's and Roberto's mothers work in the same office.

● A NOTE ON PLURALS ●

A common mistake is to use an apostrophe to pluralize a word. This is almost always incorrect. There are very few instances where using an apostrophe to signify a plural would be correct. These include:

Creating a plural possessive: The girls' lunches were stolen.
Plural letters of the alphabet: Shannon got four A's and two B's on her report card.

QUIZ

Circle the word that is spelled correctly.

1. *Linda's / Lindas* calendar was too small to fit all of her appointments.
2. We decided to order the hot turkey *sandwiches / sandwich's* on rye.
3. The *bus's / buses* parked in front of the school in the afternoon.
4. Those are the *hostess's / hostesses* favorite candles.
5. Did *Rudy's / Rudys* cat climb up the tree?
6. The lion bared *its / it's* huge, sharp teeth.
7. The *magistrate's /magistrates* daughter was lovely.
8. *Jones / Jones's* mother looked younger than her years.
9. The *puppy's / puppies* were so tiny; they could all fit in a shoebox.
10. We knew nothing about the *waitress' / waitresses* past.

THE GOOF-UP
RULE #16: Abbreviations

GOOF-PROOF!

Abbreviations are followed by periods except in these cases:

- *Two-letter postal code abbreviations for states*
- *Initials representing a company or agency*
- *Letters in acronyms*

oops!

What's an acronym? Acronyms are words formed from the first letters of a name, such as *SPAC* for *S*aratoga *P*erforming *A*rts Center. They also can be formed by combining the first letters or parts of a series of words, such as *radar* for *ra*dio *d*etecting *a*nd *r*anging.

● Common Abbreviations

Days	Sun., Mon., Tues., Wed., Thurs., Fri., Sat.
Months	Jan., Feb., Mar., Apr., Jun., Jul., Aug., Sept., Oct., Nov., Dec.
Titles	Ms., Mrs., Mr., Esq.
Degrees	Dr., Hon., M.D., Ph.D., Ed.D.
Rank	Pvt., Sgt., Capt., Maj., Col., Gen.

QUIZ

Write out the correct abbreviations for the following words.

1. Massachusetts
2. General Electric
3. October
4. Sunday
5. Lieutenant
6. California
7. Doctor
8. Captain
9. Junior
10. Tuesday
11. New Jersey
12. Mister
13. versus
14. public relations
15. United States of America

THE GOOF-UP
RULE #17: Heavy-Handed with Hyphens

GOOF-PROOF!

Prefixes are generally joined directly to words without the need for hyphens. Joining two or more words, however, often calls for hyphen use, especially if the created phrase will act as an adjective. There are several quick rules for using hyphens below.

Use a hyphen:

- When words are used together as one part of speech, like family relationships
    sister-in-law, editor-in-chief
- After *vice, ex,* or *self*
    self-employed, ex-husband, Vice-Chancellor
- When joining a prefix to a capitalized word
    Mid-Atlantic, post-World War I, un-American
- To make compound numbers of fractions
    one-half, two-thirds, eighty-three
- To combine numbers with nouns
    three-year-olds, fifty-cent ride, four-year term
- When forming an adjective that will appear before a noun, but not after
    first-rate hotel, five-star restaurant, well-built house
- To form ethnic designations
    Chinese-American, Indo-European

QUIZ

Circle the correct word or phrase to complete each sentence.

1. My *mother in law / mother-in-law* lives in Florida.
2. Her generosity was completely *self-serving / self serving*.
3. The depth of her depression was *unfathomable / un-fathomable* to her friends.
4. She was looking for an apartment in a *prewar / pre-war* building.
5. Cindy was proud of her *Japanese-American / Japanese American* heritage.
6. Around town, the mayor was very *well known / well-known*.
7. Sixteen *seven-year-olds / seven year olds* were on the field trip to the museum.
8. I am still friendly with my *exsupervisor / ex-supervisor*.
9. The *editor-in-chief / editor in chief* nixed my submission.
10. The chances of that are highly *unlikely / un-likely*.

THE GOOF-UP

RULE #18: Creating Compound Words— Adding a Word to a Word

GOOF-PROOF!

Putting two words together is often as simple as adding one word to the other. When determining whether or not two individual words in succession can be combined into one compound word, ask yourself if the combination creates one idea or item. If not, the words should always stay separate. For information on adding prefixes and suffixes to words, review Section One.

As you learned in the rule about the use of hyphens, there are specific instances where hyphens are used in combining words. Hyphens are used when forming adjectives that appear before a noun, for example. In creating compound words, hyphens are not used. In most cases, you will merge the two words with their spelling intact.

Here are some compound words:

notepad, notepaper, notebook	hardcover
stockpile, stockroom	bedridden
mailroom	homebound
catcall, catnap	earthbound
storehouse	homemaker
mainframe	housekeeping
laptop	houseplants
workplace, workstation, workspace	houseguest
wordplay	holidaymaker
hothead, hotfoot	uptown
paperback	downtown

QUIZ

Circle the correct word or words to complete each sentence.

1. Jennifer led the *sightseers / sight-seers* on a mountain hike.
2. I like to keep my *household / house hold* tidy and organized.
3. When I saw Tom's new laptop I thought, "Wow! What a *supercomputer / super computer!*"
4. The police targeted a radius of four blocks for a crime *crack down / crackdown*.
5. No one likes to ride with Julia because she drives like she has a *lead foot / leadfoot*.
6. The southern exposure and large windows makes this a very *hothouse / hot house*.
7. Do you know the secret *catch phrase / catch-phrase?*
8. The plane will not leave until we are all *onboard / on board*.
9. I'd like to save the *paper clips / paperclips* of my articles to CD-ROM.
10. If Vanessa's *roommate / room mate* decides to move out, I plan to move in.

THE GOOF-UP
RULE #19: Past Tense

GOOF-PROOF!

It seems simple enough—the past tense represents action that happened in the past. Often, -ed is added to a verb and, voila! Your word is now in the past tense. There are exceptions galore, however, and special nuances that you will need to learn.

Past, past progressive, past perfect, past perfect progressive. How can you goof-proof yourself against all of those tenses? Here's a rundown:

Past:	Represents action that happened in the past and requires a past form of a verb.
Past progressive:	Represents a *continuing* action in the past. Add a helping verb (like *was* or *were*) before the progressive (*-ing*) form of a verb.
Past perfect:	Represents an action completed in the past. Add the helping verb, *had* before the past participle form of a verb.
Past perfect progressive:	Represents a *continuing* action that began in the past. Add the helping verb *had been* before the progressive (*-ing*) of a verb.

For example:

Past:	I *walked* to work this morning.
Past progressive:	I *was walking* to work yesterday when it started to rain.
Past perfect:	I *had walked* to work in the rain before, so it didn't bother me.

Past perfect progressive: I *had been walking* on a daily basis for three consecutive weeks and didn't want to let the rain break my streak.

To form the past tense of a verb, you will most often add *-ed* to the end. In some cases, however, the past tense will appear to be a completely different word. It is your challenge to learn those words and their past tense forms.

Some words that take *-ed* to form the past tense:

live—lived
talk—talked
decide—decided
dress—dressed
move—moved
count—counted
print—printed
create—created
open—opened

Words that change interior vowels:

run—ran
drink—drank
write—wrote
win—won
begin—began
spit—spat
know—knew
ride—rode

Words that change form:

think—thought
buy—bought
seek—sought
pay—paid
lay—laid
say—said
go—went

Words that change a final consonant:

build—built
make—made
feel—felt
spend—spent

QUIZ

Complete the following sentences using the correct form of the verb in parentheses.

1. We were (sail) _____ all afternoon.
2. She (feel) _____ ill so she went home early.
3. They have been (write) _____ letters to each other for almost ten years.
4. I was ecstatic to learn that I (win) _____ the raffle.
5. You (speak) _____ with Rachel yesterday, right?
6. Lucy had been (think) _____ about applying to graduate school.
7. He (buy) _____ three sweaters and a pair of slacks.
8. Have you (move) _____ into your new apartment yet?
9. Richard (build) _____ the yellow birdhouse.
10. They were very hungry so they (begin) _____ dinner without me.

THE GOOF-UP
RULE #20: Commonly Confused Words

GOOF-PROOF!

Pay attention to the meaning of every word that you use in your writing. If you are unsure that the word you are using is correct, look it up in your dictionary (or refer to the list below of commonly confused words).

When you misuse words, your writing suffers. One wrong word—using *illicit* when you mean *elicit*, for example—can completely change the meaning of an otherwise well-written letter. If your incorrect usage appears in a resume or cover letter you sent in an application for a new job, you could ruin your chance for employment with that company.

The list provided here contains some of the most commonly confused words, along with a brief definition of each. Some of the words below are homophones, which you read about in Section One. Do yourself a favor and learn all the words below, as well as the homophone list in Section One, and practice using them correctly. As you read through the lists, ask yourself if you are guilty of incorrectly using any of the words. If you are, make a list of your personal confusing words. Spend extra time learning the words on your list (flash cards will come in handy here, too!).

CONFUSING WORDS	QUICK DEFINITION
accept	recognize
except	excluding
access	means of approaching
excess	extra
adapt	to adjust
adopt	to take as one's own
affect	to influence
effect (noun)	result
effect (verb)	to bring about

CONFUSING WORDS	QUICK DEFINITION
all ready	totally prepared
already	by this time
allude	make an indirect reference to
elude	evade
illusion	unreal appearance
all ways	every method
always	forever
among	in the middle of several
between	in an interval separating (two)
appraise	to establish value
apprise	to inform
assure	to make certain (assure someone)
ensure	to make certain
insure	to make certain (financial value)
beside	next to
besides	in addition to
bibliography	list of writings
biography	a life story
breath	respiration
breathe	to inhale and exhale
breadth	width
capital (noun)	money
capital (adjective)	most important
capitol	government building
complement	match
compliment	praise
continual	constantly
continuous	uninterrupted
decent	well-mannered
descent	decline, fall
disburse	to pay
disperse	to spread out
disinterested	no strong opinion either way
uninterested	don't care
elicit	to stir up
illicit	illegal

CONFUSING WORDS	QUICK DEFINITION
eminent	well known
imminent	pending
envelop	surround
envelope	paper wrapping for a letter
farther	beyond
further	additional
immigrate	enter a new country
emigrate	leave a country
imply	hint, suggest
infer	assume, deduce
incredible	beyond belief, astonishing
incredulous	skeptical, disbelieving
loose	not tight
lose	unable to find
may be	something may possibly be
maybe	perhaps
overdo	do too much
overdue	late
persecute	to mistreat
prosecute	to take legal action
personal	individual
personnel	employees
precede	go before
proceed	continue
proceeds	profits
principal (adjective)	main
principal (noun)	person in charge
principle	standard
stationary	still, not moving
stationery	writing material
than	in contrast to
then	next
their	belonging to them
there	in a place
they're	they are

CONFUSING WORDS	QUICK DEFINITION
weather	climate
whether	if
who	substitute for he, she, or they
whom	substitute for him, her, or them
your	belonging to you
you're	you are

QUIZ

Circle the correct word to complete each sentence.

1. David's office is on the first floor of the *capital / capitol.*
2. I had to pay $1.65 in fines for my *overdue / overdo* library books.
3. Louise *emigrated / immigrated* to Canada when she was seven.
4. He had the ring *apprised / appraised* for insurance purposes.
5. She selected the heavy stock for her *stationary / stationery.*
6. I *assured / ensured* Rebecca that her new hairstyle was attractive.
7. *There / Their* sofa was delivered this morning.
8. The yellow dress fits better *then / than* the red one.
9. The *personal / personnel* office is in the back of the building.
10. He *alluded / eluded* the police for thirteen days before being caught.

THE GOOF-UP
RULE #21: *Mon Dieu!* Foreign Language Words Buck All the Rules!

GOOF-PROOF!

Aside from learning the foreign languages of the words that confuse you, your best bet for improving your spelling of often-used foreign language words is to practice, practice, practice, and commit the spelling of your chosen words to memory.

You may shy away from using words from other languages in your writing because you fear spelling them incorrectly. It is an understandable fear, but one that you can overcome. If you choose a few select words to learn, you can use them with great impact. And that is why words from other languages have found their way into English—because they make an impact that an English word simply cannot.

Starting with the words provided here, you can begin to fashion a list of your own high-impact foreign language words. If you are unfamiliar with these words, look them up in your dictionary.

WORD	WATCH OUT!
aficionado	Only one *f*, tricky *cio* combination
avant-garde	Words are hyphenated
blasé	Accent on the *e*
bourgeois	Tricky second syllable: *geois*
cliché	Accent on the *e*
debut	Silent *t*
élan	Starts with an *e*, not an *a*
entrepreneur	Ending is *eur* not *ure*
epitome	Ends in *e*, not *y*
fait accompli	Two words, first is not *fet*
gauche	Vowel combination is *au*, not *ow*
imbroglio	Don't forget the *g*
ingénue	Starts with an *i*, not an *e*
laissez-faire	Two words, hyphenated

WORD	WATCH OUT!
malaise	Tricky second syllable: *laise*
naïve	Vowel combination is *aï,* not *ai*
non sequitur	Two words, second one ends in *ur,* not *our*
oeuvre	Tricky *oeu* combination
rendezvous	One word
vendetta	Double *t*
vignette	Don't forget the *g*

QUIZ

Circle the correctly spelled word in each of the following sentences.

1. Coco Chanel was the *epitomee / epitome* of style.
2. Marilyn wore youthful attire for her performance as the *engénue / ingénue* in the play.
3. Her mother wore a *gauche / goche* caftan to the party.
4. My supervisor believes in *laissez-faire / laisez faire* management.
5. We all wondered who would be awarded the *Entrepreneur / Entrepernure* of the Year award.

THE GOOF-UP
RULE #22: Learning Legal Terms

GOOF-PROOF!

Don't be intimidated by legal terms. If you adopt the attitude that you can learn them, you will. Then, do so by studying the list provided here, and using legal resources to familiarize yourself with the terms.

A couple of ways to get yourself familiarized with legal terms is to visit legal websites and to read legal documents such as leases, credit card agreements, or mortgage contracts. Read a document through, writing out any words with which you are not familiar. Look those words up in your dictionary, learn the definitions, and read over the document again, paying close attention to the terms you just learned. After you've become more familiar with the meaning of the legal terms, you can begin to focus on learning how to spell them. Employ the mnemonics techniques outlined in Section Two, or use flash cards, for example.

Here is a list of commonly used legal terms to get you started. Read through the terms and then find each one in your dictionary. Write out the meaning so you can learn what the words mean, along with how to spell them.

WORD	WATCH OUT!
abrogate	One *b* and one *r*
adjudicate	Don't forget the *d* in the first syllable
appellate	Double *p* and double *l*
affidavit	It's *affi-* not *affa-*
bequest	Spelled like it sounds
contraband	Prefix is *contra-* not *contro-*
deposition	Don't mistake this with *disposition*
exhume	Don't forget the *h*
extradite	Spelled like it sounds

WORD	WATCH OUT!
intestate	Not to be confused with *interstate*!
ipso facto	Two words, no hyphen
larceny	One *n*
lien	Not *lean*
litigious	Tricky last syllable: *gious*
jurisprudence	One word
malfeasance	Ending is -*ance*, not -*ence*
perjury	*per* not *pur*
plagiarism	Don't forget the first *i*
sanction	Don't forget the *t*
tort	No *e* on the end

QUIZ

Circle the correctly spelled term in the following sentences.

1. If I give a *desposition / deposition*, I may not have to testify in court.
2. The last thing she wanted to do was commit *perjury / purjury* while under oath.
3. Who will *adjudicate / ajudicate* the case?
4. The car thief was caught and charged with *larceny / larseny*.
5. He was denied a new loan because of the existing *lein / lien* on his business.
6. Brenda said she is appalled that we have become such a *litigious / litigous* society.
7. Although her children thought she had prepared a will, Mrs. Smith actually died *intestate / intastate*.
8. The *sanctions / sancsions* against the tiny country were lifted.

9. The trial was moved to an *applet / appellate* court.
10. The defendant had a signed *affadavid / affidavit* as evidence for his case.

THE GOOF-UP
RULE #23: Bumbling over Business Terms

GOOF-PROOF!

If you do not know how to spell a word that you are using in busi-ness correspondence, stop immediately and pick up your diction-ary. Misspellings in the workplace are a quick way to make a poor impression. You can improve your spelling of business terms by learning the list in this section and by reading business journals, magazines, books, and checking out websites.

Business books are excellent resources for learning to spell busi-ness terms because they often include glossaries to augment their content. Business magazines and websites usually feature timely topics and will make use of current terms or "buzzwords." Learn-ing the proper usage and spelling of buzzwords can be quite ben-eficial to your career.

There are hundreds, if not thousands, of business sites on the Internet. Here is a short list to get you started:

Barron's Online: www.barrons.com

Bloomberg.com: www.bloomberg.com (includes a financial glossary at: www.bloomberg.com/money/tools/bfglosa.html)

Business Journals: www.bizjournals.com (you can personalize the site to your locality)

Business Week Online: www.businessweek.com

Career Journal from The Wall Street Journal: www.careerjournal.com

CNNfn Online: www.cnnfn.com

Fast Company Magazine Online: www.fastcompany.com

Hoover's Online: www.hoovers.com

Inc. Magazine Online: www.inc.com

Office.com: www.office.com

The Business Search Engine: www.business.com

The Wall Street Journal Online: www.wsj.com

The following list includes some commonly used business terms. Read through the terms and then find each one in your dictionary. Write out the meaning so you can learn what the words mean, along with how to spell them.

WORD	WATCH OUT!
acquisition	*qui* combination in second syllable
arbitrage	Last syllable is *trage*, not *tage*
architecture	*ure* ending
beneficiary	Don't forget the second *i*
capital	Not *capitol*
collusion	Double *l*
commercial	Double *m*
consortium	*tium* ending
consumer	Ending is *-er* not *-or*
deduction	Single *d* in second syllable
disclosure	*ure* ending
discrimination	Single consonants throughout
entitlement	Don't forget the second *e*
equity	*ity* not *aty*
exempt	Don't forget the *p*
financial	Ending is *-ial*
fiscal	Single *s*, single *c*
forecast	Don't forget the *e*
franchise	Ending is *-ise* not *-ize*
harassment	Single *r*, double *s*
jargon	Ending is *-on* not *-en*
liability	Ending is *-ity* not *~-aty*
nepotism	Second syllable is *po* not *pa*
organization	*z* not *s*
perquisite	*per* not *pur* or *pre*
prospectus	Ending is *-us*
revenue	Second syllable is *ve*
subsidy	Second syllable is *si*
tenure	Single *n*, single *r*

[*QUIZ*]

Mark the following words as correct or incorrect with a check.

	CORRECT	INCORRECT
1. forcast	_____	_____
2. harass	_____	_____
3. consumer	_____	_____
4. arbitrage	_____	_____
5. benficiary	_____	_____
6. revenue	_____	_____
7. fiscally	_____	_____
8. exemt	_____	_____
9. acquisition	_____	_____
10. collussion	_____	_____
11. equaty	_____	_____
12. subsidies	_____	_____
13. financial	_____	_____
14. comerrcial	_____	_____
15. nepitism	_____	_____

THE GOOF-UP
RULE #24: Tripping over Technology Terms

GOOF-PROOF!

The technology sector has added many new words to the English language. To become more comfortable spelling these words, you will need to first become familiar with them. Approach this task the same way you approached learning foreign language and business terms.

You can easily expand your knowledge of technology terms by visiting any of the several websites geared toward the high-tech world. Here are a few sites that you might consider visiting:

CIO Magazine Online: www.cio.com
Fast Company Magazine Online: www.fastcompany.com
Government Technology: www.govtech.net
Information Technology Association of America:
    www.itaa.org
Internet.com—The IT Resource: www.internet.com
National Institute of Standards and Technology:
    www.nist.gov
Tech Web—The Business Technology Network:
    www.techweb.com
Technology & Learning: www.techlearning.com
Technology Review (MIT): www.techreview.com
Web Services Community Portal: www.webservices.org
Webmonkey: www.hotwired.lycos.com/webmonkey
    (especially the glossary)
**Webopedia—Online Dictionary for Computer and Internet
    Terms:** www.pcwebopaedia.com/
Women in Technology International: www.witi.org

The following list includes some commonly used technology terms. Read through the terms and then find each one in your dictionary. Write out the meaning so you can learn what the words mean, along with how to spell them.

WORD	WATCH OUT!
applet	One *t*
application	Double *p*
bandwidth	One word
bitmap	One *t*
browser	One *s*
cache	Don't forget the *e*
cursor	Ending is *-or* not *-er*
database	One word
development	No *e* after the *p*
domain	No final *e*
embedded	Not *imbedded*
encryption	Don't forget the *p*
frequency	Ending is *-ency*
function	Don't forget the *c*
hardware	One word
implementation	Starts with *Im* not *In*
interactive	No hyphen
interface	No hyphen
Internet	Always capitalized
intranet	Don't confuse it with *Internet*
keyword	One word
monitor	Ending is *-or*
multimedia	No hyphen
programming	Double *m*
research	Vowel combination is *ea*
rollover	One word
server	Ending is *-er* not *-or*
software	One word
style sheet	One word

WORD	WATCH OUT!
validation	Ending is *-tion*
vector	Ending is *-or* not *-er*

QUIZ

Find the misspelled words in the passage.

Smith, Inc., is a *multimedia* design and *developement* firm with headquarters in downtown Minneapolis. We specialize in ColdFusion *programming* and system-wide *inplementation* of back-end solutions. We can create *data bases* to meet all of your needs. When we work with a new client, we perform extensive *research* to learn all aspects of their business. We will investigate your *server* environment, *bandwith* limitations, data *validation* requirements, and other *soft-ware* or *hard-ware* needs.

Our designers have created exciting user *innerfaces* for companies small and large. We are adept at developing fun *applets,* splashy *roll-overs*, and other *funtions* that will keep visitors coming to your site again and again. If you are looking for a secure site, we have *programers* who specialize in *encryption*. Let Smith, Inc. be your *interactive* resource!

THE GOOF-UP
RULE #25: Literary Terms—
Not Just for English 101!

GOOF-PROOF!

Yes, you'll use literary terms to discuss the new book you read for your monthly book club. But you also can use many literary terms in your everyday writing and speaking. Using these terms can enrich your correspondence—both personal and business. However, if you use the terms and misspell them, watch out!

You probably were first introduced to literary terms in school. Perhaps you learned about *genres, irony,* and *figurative language.* Maybe you discussed the *anthropomorphism* of the roses in a particular sonnet. All of these terms have meaning outside of the realm of literature and language. Using them well, and spelling them correctly, will enhance your writing and enable you to convey a greater degree of meaning with every sentence.

You can easily expand your knowledge of literary terms by reading study guides for popular literary fiction, journals dedicated to the study of literary theory, or anthologies that include study guides or lessons. Read the book reviews in your local newspaper or your favorite magazines to pick up a few new words. There also are several websites geared toward literature, language, and literary theory. A few sites that you might consider visiting include:

Glossary of Literary Criticism:
  www.sil.org/~radneyr/humanities/litcrit/gloss.htm
Glossary of Rhetorical Terms with Examples:
  www.uky.edu/ArtsSciences/Classics/rhetoric.html
Literary Arts, Inc.: www.literary-arts.org/
Literary Criticism on the Web: http://start.at/literarycriticism
Literary Terms: www.tnellen.com/cybereng/lit_terms/
Online Literary Criticism Collection: www.ipl.org/ref/litcrit/
The Literary Web: www.people.virginia.edu/~jbh/litweb.html

Virtual Salt—A Glossary of Literary Terms:
www.virtualsalt.com/litterms.htm
Wordwizard: www.wordwizard.com
Zuzu's Petals Literary Resources: www.zuzu.com

The following list includes several commonly used literary terms. Read through the terms and then find each one in your dictionary. Write out the meaning so you can learn what the words mean, along with how to spell them.

WORD	WATCH OUT!
allusion	Double *l*
analogy	Ending is *-ogy*
anthropomorphism	Break it down—this one is tough!
canon	Single *n*
conceit	Ending is *-eit* not *-ete*
conflict	Don't forget the *t*
connotation	Double *n*
epistolary	Starts with *e* not *a*
foreshadowing	Not forshadowing
genre	Ending is *-re* not *-er*
hyperbole	Ending is *-e* not *-y*
infer	Single *r*
invective	Not *invictive*
irony	Spelled like it sounds
metaphor	*ph* not *f*
motif	Ends in a single *f*
nemesis	Second syllable is *me* not *mi*
oxymoron	No hyphen
paradox	Ends in *dox* not *docs*
parody	*paro-* not *para-*
personify	Ends in *-ify* not *-ofy*
perspective	*per-* not *pr-*
pseudonym	Begins with a *p*
rhetoric	Don't forget the *h*

WORD	WATCH OUT!
rhyme	Don't forget the *h*
satire	One *t*
sequel	Ends in *-el* not *-il*
simile	One *e*
travesty	Single *v*
trite	Single *t*

QUIZ

Find the misspelled italicized words in the passage.

Yesterday, I finished reading an *epistollary* novel, written by a writer under a *pseudonym*. It was the first time I had read anything in that *genre*. What an interesting *prespective* to have! It is not often that one has the opportunity to read people's private correspondence. The characters filled their letters with *satire* and many *metaphors*. When they were so angry at each other, they wrote harsh *invectives*. Then they would make up and write poetry for each other, filled with clever *ryhmes*. I would like this author to publish a *sequill*, so I can find out what happens to the two friends as they age. Maybe it is a *trite* idea, but I think the author could publish an entire series based on the characters' letters.

section **FOUR**

RESOURCES

● PUZZLES, ACTIVITIES, AND RESOURCES ●
TO FURTHER IMPROVE
YOUR SPELLING

Crossword puzzles—Most daily newspapers have crossword puzzles. You also can purchase crossword puzzle books. Wherever you find them, doing crossword puzzles is an excellent way to reinforce your spelling skills.

Jumbles—As with crossword puzzles, these are often found in the newspaper and in word puzzle books by themselves. Jumbles are puzzles that have the letters in a word scrambled.

Word games—Pull some family members or friends together to play word games such as Scrabble® or Boggle®. Both will put your spelling to the test.

Read—The more you read, the more you will recognize words spelled properly. Read the newspaper, magazines, books, or comics. Anything you read will help make you a better speller.

Use the Internet—Sign up to receive "Word of the Day" e-mails. These will enhance your vocabulary and increase your familiarity with the spelling of various words. One site that offers a "Word of the Day" service is www.dictionary.com.

Test yourself—Compile a Goof-Up list, consisting of words that you frequently misspell, or words that you will use often in work or school. Ask a friend to give you a weekly spelling test based on those words. Or, write out the words on your list, leaving blank spaces for some of the letters. See how many you can fill in correctly.

Turn off your spell-check function—Turning off your spell-check function will force you to proofread your writing very carefully, rather than relying on a tool that isn't all that reliable! If you are unsure whether or not you have spelled something correctly, look it up in the dictionary immediately. Taking charge of your spelling in everything you write will make you a more confident and competent speller.

● BOOKS ●

There are many other guidebooks that can help you to continue to refine your spelling skills. Consider buying or taking out of the library one or more of the following:

Agnes, Michael. *Webster's New World Pocket Misspeller's Dictionary*. New York: Hungry Minds, 1997.

Castley, Anna. *Practical Spelling: The Bad Speller's Guide to Getting It Right Every Time*. New York: Learning Express, 1998.

Dougherty, Margaret M., et al. *Instant Spelling Dictionary*. New York: Warner Books, 1990.

Downing, David. *303 Dumb Spelling Mistakes . . . and What You Can Do About Them*. New York: National Textbook Company, 1989.

Emery, Robert W. and Crosby, Harry H. *Better Spelling in 30 Minutes a Day*. New York: Career Press, 1995.

LearningExpress. *1001 Vocabulary and Spelling Questions: Fast, Focused Practice to Help You Improve Your Vocabulary and Spelling Skills*. New York: LearningExpress, 1999.

Magnan, Robert and Mary Lou Santovec. *1001 Commonly Misspelled Words: What Your Spell Checker Won't Tell You*. New York: McGraw-Hill, 2000.

Morrow, David. *DK Pockets: Spelling Dictionary*. New York: DK Publishing, 1998.

Shefter, Harry. *Six Minutes a Day to Perfect Spelling*. New York: Pocket Books, 1984.

Sorsby, Claudia. *Spelling 101*. New York: St. Martin's, 1996.

vos Savant, Marilyn. *The Art of Spelling: The Method and the Madness*. New York: W.W. Norton & Company, 2000.

● TROUBLESOME WORDS ●

The following list represents 150 words that are often misspelled. Each word presented is spelled correctly. As you read through this list, you may find yourself surprised at the spelling. There are people who have been writing *calandar, jewelery,* or *millenium* for years and they are quite shocked when they see the correct spelling!

You can goof-proof yourself against misspelling these troublesome words by becoming familiar with their correct spelling. First, read through the list and check each word that has surprising spelling. Then, write out each of those words that you think you regularly misspell. Look over your list and think about the Goof-Proof rules that apply to each word. Notice any patterns? Do you have a tough time with double consonants? Are plurals your weakness? If you see patterns emerge, spend some extra time on the Goof-Proof rules that apply.

1. absence
2. abundance
3. accidentally
4. accommodate
5. acknowledgment
6. acquaintance
7. aggravate
8. alibi
9. alleged
10. ambiguous
11. analysis
12. annual
13. argument
14. awkward
15. basically
16. boundary
17. bulletin
18. calendar
19. canceled
20. cannot
21. cemetery
22. coincidence
23. collectible
24. committee
25. comparative
26. completely
27. condemn
28. congratulations
29. conscientious
30. consistent
31. convenient
32. correspondence
33. deceive
34. definitely
35. dependent
36. depot
37. descend
38. desperate
39. development
40. dilemma
41. discrepancy
42. eighth
43. eligible
44. embarrass
45. equivalent
46. euphoria
47. existence
48. exuberance
49. feasible
50. February
51. fifth
52. forcibly
53. forfeit
54. formerly
55. fourth
56. fulfill
57. grateful
58. grievance
59. guarantee
60. guidance
61. harass
62. hindrance
63. ideally
64. implement
65. independence
66. indispensable
67. inoculate
68. insufficient
69. interference
70. interrupt
71. jealousy
72. jewelry
73. judgment
74. leisure
75. length
76. lenient

77. liaison
78. lieutenant
79. lightning
80. loophole
81. losing
82. maintenance
83. maneuver
84. mathematics
85. millennium
86. minuscule
87. miscellaneous
88. misspell
89. negotiable
90. ninth
91. occasionally
92. occurred
93. omission
94. opportunity
95. outrageous
96. pamphlet
97. parallel
98. perceive
99. permanent
100. perseverance
101. personnel
102. possess
103. potato
104. precede
105. preferred
106. prejudice
107. prevalent
108. privilege
109. procedure
110. proceed
111. prominent
112. pronunciation
113. quandary

114. questionnaire
115. receipt
116. receive
117. recommend
118. reference
119. referred
120. regardless
121. relevant
122. religious
123. remembrance
124. reservoir
125. responsible
126. restaurant
127. rhythm
128. ridiculous
129. roommate
130. scary
131. scissors
132. secretary
133. separate
134. souvenir
135. specifically
136. sufficient
137. supersede
138. temperament
139. temperature
140. truly
141. twelfth
142. ubiquitous
143. unanimous
144. usually
145. usurp
146. vacuum
147. vengeance
148. visible
149. Wednesday
150. wherever

ANSWER KEY

● INTRODUCTION ●

The correct sentences are:

I work from home on *Mondays*, *Wednesdays*, and *Fridays*.
Lucy asked her hairdresser for a low *maintenance* cut.
As a *secretary*, she regularly used a spreadsheet program.

● PRETEST ●

1. *Independence* was spelled correctly.
2. Incorrect. The correct spelling is *parallel*.
3. *Receive* was spelled correctly.
4. *Absence* was spelled correctly.
5. *Achieve* was spelled correctly.
6. Incorrect. The correct spelling is *globally*.
7. *Support* was spelled correctly.
8. *Ridiculous* was spelled correctly.
9. Incorrect. The correct spelling is *immediately*.
10. *Usually* was spelled correctly.

11. *Wednesday* was spelled correctly.
12. Incorrect. The correct spelling is *terrible*.
13. *Permanent* was spelled correctly.
14. Incorrect. The correct spelling is *manner*.
15. Incorrect. The correct spelling is *calamity*.
16. *Courage* was spelled correctly.
17. *Decision* was spelled correctly.
18. *Fewer* was spelled correctly.
19. Incorrect. The correct spelling is *pursue*.
20. *Millennium* was spelled correctly.
21. *Fourth* was spelled correctly.
22. Incorrect. The correct spelling is *grammar*.
23. *Especially* was spelled correctly.
24. *Necessary* was spelled correctly.
25. Incorrect. The correct spelling is *frequent*.
26. *Eight* was spelled correctly.
27. Incorrect. The correct spelling is *consistency*.
28. *Perceive* was spelled correctly.
29. *Liaison* was spelled correctly.
30. Incorrect. The correct spelling is *category*.
31. Incorrect. The correct spelling is *harass*.
32. Incorrect. The correct spelling is *fundamental*.
33. *Stopped* was spelled correctly.
34. *Cheap* was spelled correctly.
35. Incorrect. The correct spelling is *reference*.
36. *Balance* was spelled correctly.
37. Incorrect. The correct spelling is *jewelry*.
38. *Committee* was spelled correctly.
39. Incorrect. The correct spelling is *intramural*.
40. *Thinking* was spelled correctly.
41. *Correction* was spelled correctly.
42. Incorrect. The correct spelling is *survival*.
43. *Simultaneous* was spelled correctly.
44. *Punctuate* was spelled correctly.
45. Incorrect. The correct spelling is *leveling*.
46. Incorrect. The correct spelling is *a lot*.
47. Incorrect. The correct spelling is *existence*.
48. *Proclaim* was spelled correctly.

49. *Generate* was spelled correctly.
50. Incorrect. The correct spelling is *anonymous.*

● SECTION ONE ●

● Roots

Quiz I
Match the root with the correct meaning.

1. *agon* = **g**, to struggle.
    Agony is a personal *struggle.*
2. *tract* = **f**, draw.
    When you are at**tract**ed to something, you are *drawn* to it.
3. *greg* = **i**, crowd.
    A **greg**arious person is usually very sociable; he likes to be part of the *crowd.*
4. *bio* = **c,** life.
    Biology is the science of *life.*
5. *ten* = **j**, to hold
    A **ten**acious person *holds* fast to a belief or goal.
6. *contra* = **b**, to oppose.
    To **contra**dict is to support an *opposing* view or stance on an issue.
7. *ject* = **e**, to throw.
    The e**ject**ion seat *throws* a pilot out of a plane (with a parachute!) in an emergency.
8. *phil* = **a**, love.
    Philanthropy is a *love* for humanity.
9. *dem* = **h**, people
    A **dem**ocracy is a type government ruled by the *people.*
10. *soph* = **d**, wisdom.
    Philo**soph**ers spend their lives in the pursuit of *wisdom.*

Quiz II
Circle the root in the following words.

1. (cred)ential
2. (trib)utary
3. im(ped)iment
4. biblio(phile)
5. (aud)itory
6. con(tract)
7. (phob)ia
8. (ben)efit
9. (simul)taneous
10. (vid)eo

● Prefixes

Quiz
Circle the correct prefix used in each of the following sentences.

1. Sylvia was (*disheartened*) to learn that she was wait-listed at State University.
2. The (*pretest*) was difficult for everyone because they hadn't yet learned algebra.
3. Stealing was (*antithetical*) to her beliefs.
4. He felt constant pain in his arm after (*hyperextending*) his elbow.
5. The meteorologist called for (*intermittent*) rain.

Suffixes

Quiz
Circle the correct part of speech for each suffix.

-ist	noun
-ify	verb
-ology	noun
-ile	adjective
-tion	noun
-able	adjective
-ious	adjective
-less	adjective
-ize	verb
-ism	noun
-ic	adjective

Homophones

Quiz
Complete the sentences by circling the correct homophone.

1. The (two) girls were shopping for prom dresses.
2. She couldn't (bear) to see her son cry.
3. We waited outside for hours just to get a sneak (peek.)
4. Emily was thrilled that she (passed) her French exam.
5. He wanted a buzz-cut to (alter) his appearance.
6. Are we meeting once or twice a (week)?
7. We'll decide what to do after (roll) call.
8. I had to stop running after I hurt my (heel.)
9. I don't like the (coarse) texture of corn bread.
10. Tom carried the (pail) of water for two miles.

❖ SECTION TWO ❖

❖ Rule #1
When to use *IE* and *EI*

Your circled words should match the circled words here. The mis-spelled words in the exercise are corrected below.

1. (friend)
2. (receipt)
3. sleigh
4. conceit
5. (receive)
6. (sleight)
7. (weight)
8. (achieve)
9. seize
10. (believe)
11. grievous
12. heinous
13. (mischievous)
14. piece
15. relief
16. (yield)
17. chief
18. perceive

❖ Rule #2
When to Use *IA* and *AI*

1. menial
2. certain
3. fountain
4. familiar
5. Britain
6. alleviate
7. judicial

8. Martian
9. Indian
10. curtain
11. auxiliary
12. guardian
13. mountain
14. substantial
15. captain
16. immediately
17. controversial
18. artificial

Rule #3
Overwhelming Vowel Combinations

1. paisley
2. juice
3. nuisance
4. conceal
5. prevail
6. refrain
7. menial
8. certain
9. dreary
10. mountain

• Rule #4
Doubling Final Consonants

	YES	NO
1. meet		✔
2. mop	✔	
3. look		✔
4. seal		✔
5. drink		✔
6. bet	✔	
7. discover		✔
8. clap	✔	
9. pump		✔
10. walk		✔

• Rule #6
The Hard and Soft Sides of the Letter C

1. In biology class, she learned about the life *cycle* of butter-flies.
2. You can save money at the grocery store if you use *coupons*.
3. Harry became an actor because he loved being the *center* of attention.
4. Who *caused* the fire?
5. He bought a new pair of hedge *clippers*.

Rule #7
"*G*" Whiz! *G* Can Be Soft or Hard, Too!

1. In *general*, Roxanne was pleased with her results.
2. Climbing the mountain was a *gutsy* thing to do.
3. The *guys* waited for Brian at the front entrance.
4. The family liked to see the *giraffes* at the zoo.
5. Elsa's brother had the flu, and she was afraid of catching his *germs*.

Plurals Pretest

If you misspelled this plural, go to the following rule.

1. child = children	Rule #9: Pesky Plurals
2. stereo = stereos	Rule #8: Regular Plurals
3. tomato = tomatoes	Rule #8: Regular Plurals
4. gulf = gulfs	Rule #10: Funky *F*
5. computer = computers	Rule #8: Regular Plurals
6. pantry = pantries	Rule #12: Final *Y*
7. medium = media	Rule #9: Pesky Plurals
8. syllabus = syllabi	Rule #9: Pesky Plurals
9. sweater = sweaters	Rule #8: Regular Plurals
10. decoy = decoys	Rule #12: Final *Y*
11. knife = knives	Rule #10: Funky *F*
12. man = men	Rule #9: Pesky Plurals
13. self = selves	Rule #10: Funky *F*
14. piano = pianos	Rule #8: Regular Plurals
15. parenthesis = parentheses	Rule #9: Pesky Plurals
16. lunch = lunches	Rule #8: Regular Plurals
17. stress = stresses	Rule #8: Regular Plurals
18. rally = rallies	Rule #12: Final *Y*
19. apex = apices	Rule #9: Pesky Plurals
20. curriculum = curricula	Rule #9: Pesky Plurals

Rule #8
Regular Plurals—When to Just Add -s and When to Add -es

SINGULAR	PLURAL
1. box	boxes
2. watch	watches
3. radio	radios
4. sandwich	sandwiches
5. dress	dresses
6. television	televisions
7. calendar	calendars
8. potato	potatoes
9. cookie	cookies
10. guess	guesses

Rule #9
Pesky Plurals

SINGULAR	PLURAL
1. phenomenon	phenomena
2. focus	foci
3. stimulus	stimuli
4. child	children
5. oasis	oases
6. alumnus	alumni
7. woman	women
8. analysis	analyses
9. bacterium	bacteria
10. ellipsis	ellipses

Rule #10
The Funky *F*— Making Words Plural
When They End in *f* or *fe*

SINGULAR	PLURAL
1. self	selves
2. hoof	hooves
3. wolf	wolves
4. thief	thieves
5. chef	chefs
6. gulf	gulfs
7. wife	wives
8. elf	elves
9. belief	beliefs
10. loaf	loaves

Rule #11
When to Drop a Final *E*

1. true + ly = truly
2. browse + ed = browsed
3. peace + able = peaceable
4. change + ing = changing
5. opportune + ity = opportunity
6. surprise + ing = surprising
7. argue + able = arguable
8. encourage + ing = encouraging
9. able + ly = ably
10. fake + ed = faked
11. tie + ing = tying
12. advance + ing = advancing
13. bake + ing = baking
14. singe + ing = singeing
15. grace + ful =graceful

Rule #12
When to Keep a Final *Y*—When to Change It to *I*

1. holy + ness = holiness
2. study + ing = studying
3. comply + s = complies
4. sully + ed = sullied
5. carry + ing = carrying
6. destroy + ed = destroyed
7. say + ing = saying
8. drowsy + ness = drowsiness
9. funny + er = funnier
10. queasy + ness = queasiness
12. likely + er = likelier
13. decay + s = decays
14. tidy + er = tidier
15. runny + ness = runniness
16. spy + ing = spying

Rule #13
Adding Endings to Words that End with a *C*

1. Peter would spend entire afternoons *mimicking* his sister.
2. Whenever she rode on a roller coaster she would become *panicky*.
3. We were relieved when the drug *traffickers* were arrested.
4. She had a distinct, easily *mimicked* voice.
5. In the summer, they would go on many *picnics*.
6. Anna had trouble learning to read until her mother started helping her with *phonics*.
7. You can get by in a foreign country as long as you know the *basics* of the language.
8. Parts of Boston have a very *historical* feel.
9. The barbarians *havocked* Rome.
10. The wire was *electrically* charged.

Rule #14
Apostrophes—The Attraction of Contractions

1. *We're* heading out to the beach.
2. *Don't* eat that cake, *it's* for Harold!
3. *She's* baking cookies.
4. *They're* studying hard for the exam tomorrow.
5. *It's* a bright sunny day.
6. Jeremy thinks that *I'm* keeping secrets!
7. Harriet *doesn't* like fish and chips.
8. Take off *your* boots if *you've* been outside.
9. I *won't* eat liver.
10. I *wouldn't* go to Sylvia's if you paid me!

Rule #15
Apostrophes—The Politics of Possessives

1. *Linda's* calendar was too small to fit all of her appointments.
2. We decided to order the hot turkey *sandwiches* on rye.
3. The *buses* parked in front of the school in the afternoon.
4. Those are the *hostess's* favorite candles.
5. Did *Rudy's* cat climb up the tree?
6. The lion bared *its* huge, sharp teeth.
7. The *magistrate's* daughter was lovely.
8. *Jones's* mother looked younger than her years.
9. The *puppies* were so tiny; they could all fit in a shoebox.
10. We knew nothing about the *waitress'* past.

Rule #16
Abbreviations

FULL NAME OR WORD	ABBREVIATION
1. Massachusetts	MA
2. General Electric	GE
3. October	Oct.
4. Sunday	Sun.
5. Lieutenant	Lieut.
6. California	CA
7. Doctor	Dr.
8. Captain	Capt.
9. Junior	Jr.
10. Tuesday	Tues.
11. New Jersey	NJ
12. Mister	Mr.
13. versus	vs.
14. public relations	P.R.
15. United States of America	USA

Rule #17
Heavy-Handed with Hyphens

1. My *mother-in-law* lives in Florida.
2. Her generosity was completely *self-serving*.
3. The depth of her depression was *unfathomable* to her friends.
4. She was looking for an apartment in a *prewar* building.
5. Cindy was proud of her *Japanese-American* heritage.
6. Around town, the mayor was very *well known*.
7. Sixteen *seven-year-olds* were on the field trip to the museum.
8. I am still friendly with my *ex-supervisor*.
9. The *editor-in-chief* nixed my submission.
10. The chances of that are highly *unlikely*.

Rule #18
Creating Compound Words—
Adding a Word to a Word

1. Jennifer led the *sightseers* on a mountain hike.
2. I like to keep my *household* organized and tidy.
3. When I saw Tom's new laptop I thought, "Wow! What a *super computer!*"
4. The police targeted a radius of four blocks for a crime *crackdown*.
5. No one likes to ride with Julia because she drives like she has a *lead foot*.
6. The southern exposure and large windows makes this a very *hot house*.
7. Do you know the secret *catchphrase*?
8. The plane will not leave until we are all *on board*.
9. I'd like to save the *paper clips* of my articles to CD-ROM.
10. If Vanessa's *roommate* decides to move out, I plan to move in.

Rule #19
Past Tense

1. We were *sailing* all afternoon.
2. She *felt* ill so she went home.
3. They have been *writing* letters to each other for almost ten years.
4. I was ecstatic to learn that I *won* the raffle.
5. You *spoke* with Rhonda yesterday, right?
6. Lucy had been *thinking* about applying to graduate school.
7. He *bought* three sweaters and a pair of slacks.
8. Have you *moved* into your new apartment yet?
9. Richard *built* the yellow birdhouse.
10. They were very hungry so they *began* dinner without me.

Rule #20
Commonly Confused Words

1. David's office is on the first floor of the *capitol*.
2. I had to pay $1.65 in fines for my *overdue* library books.
3. Louise *immigrated* to Canada when she was seven.
4. He had the ring *appraised* for insurance purposes.
5. She selected the heavy stock for her *stationery*.
6. I *assured* Rebecca that her new hairstyle was attractive.
7. *Their* sofa was delivered this morning.
8. The yellow dress fits better *than* the red one.
9. The *personnel* office is in the back of the building.
10. He *eluded* the police for thirteen days before being caught.

Rule #21
Mon Dieu! Foreign Language Words
Buck All the Rules!

1. Coco Chanel was the *epitome* of style.
2. Marilyn wore youthful attire for her performance as the *ingénue* in the play.
3. Her mother wore a *gauche* caftan to the party.
4. My supervisor believes in *laissez-faire* management.
5. We all wondered who would be awarded the *Entrepreneur* of the Year award.

Rule #22
Learning Legal Terms

1. If I give a *deposition*, I may not have to testify in court.
2. The last thing she wanted to do was commit *perjury* while under oath.
3. Who will *adjudicate* the case?
4. The car thief was caught and charged with *larceny*.
5. He was denied a new loan because of the existing *lien* on his business.
6. Brenda said she is appalled that we have become such a *litigious* society.
7. Although her children thought she had prepared a will, Mrs. Smith actually died *intestate*.
8. The *sanctions* against the tiny country were lifted.
9. The trial was moved to an *appellate* court.
10. The defendant had a signed *affidavit* as evidence for his case.

Rule #23
Bumbling over Business Terms

1. Incorrect. The correct spelling is *forecast*.
2. *Harass* was spelled correctly.
3. *Consumer* was spelled correctly.
4. *Arbitrage* was spelled correctly.
5. Incorrect. The correct spelling is *beneficiary*.
6. *Revenue* was spelled correctly.
7. *Fiscally* was spelled correctly.
8. Incorrect. The correct spelling is *exempt*.
9. *Acquisition* was spelled correctly.
10. Incorrect. The correct spelling is *collusion*.
11. Incorrect. The correct spelling is *equity*.
12. *Subsidies* was spelled correctly.
13. *Financial* was spelled correctly.
14. Incorrect. The correct spelling is *commercial*.
15. Incorrect. The correct spelling is *nepotism*.

- ## Rule #24
  ### Tripping over Technology Terms

1. *Multimedia* was spelled correctly.
2. Incorrect. The correct spelling is *development.*
3. *Programming* was spelled correctly.
4. Incorrect. The correct spelling is *implementation.*
5. Incorrect. The correct spelling is *databases.*
6. *Research* was spelled correctly.
7. *Server* was spelled correctly.
8. *Incorrect.* The correct spelling is *bandwidth.*
9. *Validation* was spelled correctly.
10. Incorrect. The correct spelling is *software.*
11. Incorrect. The correct spelling is *hardware.*
12. Incorrect. The correct spelling is *interfaces.*
13. *Applets* was spelled correctly.
14. Incorrect. The correct spelling is *rollovers.*
15. Incorrect. The correct spelling is *functions.*
16. Incorrect. The correct spelling is *programmers.*
17. *Encryption* was spelled correctly.
18. *Interactive* was spelled correctly.

- ## Rule #25
  ### Literary Terms—Not Just for English 101!

1. Incorrect. The correct spelling is *epistolary.*
2. *Pseudonym* was spelled correctly.
3. *Genre* was spelled correctly.
4. Incorrect. The correct spelling is *perspective.*
5. *Satire* was spelled correctly.
6. *Metaphors* was spelled correctly.
7. *Invectives* was spelled correctly.
8. Incorrect. The correct spelling is *rhymes.*
9. Incorrect. The correct spelling is *sequel.*
10. *Trite* was spelled correctly.